BABIES AT THE ZOO
Sloth Babies

Susan H. Gray

CHERRY LAKE PRESS

Published in the United States of America by
Cherry Lake Publishing
2395 South Huron Parkway, Suite 200, Ann Arbor, MI 48104
www.cherrylakepublishing.com

Content Advisor: Dominique A. Didier, Professor of Biology, Millersville University
Reading Advisor: Marla Conn, MS, Ed, Literacy specialist, Read-Ability, Inc.

Photo credits: ©Kevin Wells Photography/Shutterstock.com, front cover; ©Parkol/Shutterstock.com, 1, 2; ©Daniel Hearn/Shutterstock.com, 4; ©seubsai/Shutterstock.com, 6; ©JT Platt/Shutterstock.com, 8; ©Okan Ataman/Shutterstock.com, 10; ©kungverylucky/Shutterstock.com, 12; ©KARI K/Shutterstock.com, 14; ©ChisholmJA/Shutterstock.com, 16; ©Reimar/Shutterstock.com, 18; ©JohannesOehl/Shutterstock.com, 20

Library of Congress Cataloging-in-Publication Data

Names: Gray, Susan Heinrichs, author.
Title: Sloth babies / written by Susan H. Gray.
Description: Ann Arbor, Michigan : Cherry Lake Publishing, 2020. | Series: Babies at the zoo | Includes index. | Audience: Grades K-1.
Summary: "Read about the slow, sleepy sloth babies and the healthy meals that zookeepers provide for them. This level 3 guided reader book includes intriguing facts and adorable photos. Students will develop word recognition and reading skills while learning about how these baby animals learn and grow, what they eat, and how they socialize with each other. Book includes table of contents, glossary, index, author biographies, sidebars, and word list for home and school connection"—Provided by publisher.
Identifiers: LCCN 2019034143 (print) | LCCN 2019034144 (ebook) | ISBN 9781534158979 (hardcover) | ISBN 9781534161276 (paperback) | ISBN 9781534160125 (pdf) | ISBN 9781534162426 (ebook)
Subjects: LCSH: Sloths—Infancy—Juvenile literature. | Zoo animals—Infancy—Juvenile literature.
Classification: LCC QL737.E2 G735 2020 (print) | LCC QL737.E2 (ebook) | DDC 599.3/131392—dc23
LC record available at https://lccn.loc.gov/2019034143
LC ebook record available at https://lccn.loc.gov/2019034144

Cherry Lake Publishing would like to acknowledge the work of the Partnership for 21st Century Learning, a Network of Battelle for Kids. Please visit http://www.battelleforkids.org/networks/p21 for more information.

Printed in the United States of America
Corporate Graphics

Table of Contents

About the Author

Susan H. Gray has a master's degree in zoology. She has written more than 150 reference books for children and especially loves writing about animals. Susan lives in Cabot, Arkansas, with her husband, Michael, and many pets.

Do you think the sloth's hair feels smooth or coarse?

Slow, Sleepy Sloths

What animal moves slowly and looks green? The sloth! Sloths are slow-moving **mammals**. They live in the forests of Central and South America. Some live in zoos.

Sloths **grasp** tree limbs with their hands and feet. Then they hang upside down. Sloths eat and sleep upside down. They even give birth to their babies like this!

Mothers have one baby at a time. The baby holds tightly to its mother's fur. It lies on her chest and drinks her milk.

Sloths sleep up to 18 hours a day. Some hang from branches to sleep. Some sit or curl up in a ball.

At night, they search for food.

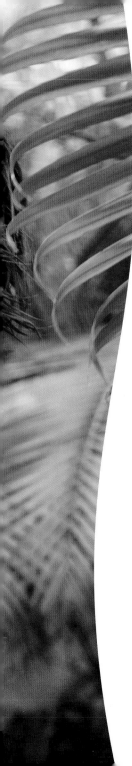

Time to Eat!

Sloths do not hear or see well. They move too slowly to hunt. But that is okay. They just want to **nibble** on leaves and fruit.

What would you make
a sloth for lunch?

At the zoo, sloths get plenty of leaves. **Zookeepers** also bring them fruits and vegetables. They even make salads for the sloths.

Going Green

Sloths will stay with their mothers for 2 to 4 years. By then, they have grown strong. They can hang from branches all day.

They have also grown long, **rough** hair. The hairs have tiny **cracks** in them. Plants called **algae** live in the cracks. The algae make the sloths look green.

At around 3 years, sloths are adults. Now they can have their own babies.

Baby sloths are born high in the trees!

Find Out More

BOOK
Bader, Bonnie. *Slow, Slow Sloths.* New York, NY: Penguin Young Readers, 2016.

WEBSITE
Memphis Zoo—Meet Our Baby Sloth!
https://www.memphiszoo.org/sloth
Learn about the baby sloth at the zoo and how it is growing up.

Glossary

algae (AL-jee) small plants without roots or stems

coarse (KORS) having a rough surface or texture

cracks (KRAKZ) narrow openings

grasp (GRASP) to hold something firmly

mammals (MAM-uhlz) animals that have hair and provide milk to their babies

nibble (NIB-uhl) to eat something by taking small bites

rough (RUFF) not smooth

zookeepers (ZOO-kee-purz) people who take care of zoo animals

Home and School Connection

Use this list of words from the book to help your child become a better reader. Word games and writing activities can help beginning readers reinforce literacy skills.

a	chest	green	long	rough	this
adults	coarse	grown	look	salads	tightly
algae	cracks	hair	looks	search	time
all	curl	hairs	lunch	see	tiny
also	day	hands	make	sit	to
America	do	hang	mammals	sleep	too
and	down	have	milk	sleepy	tree
animal	drinks	hear	mothers	sloth	trees
are	eat	her	move	sloths	up
around	even	high	moves	slow	upside
at	feels	holds	moving	slowly	vegetables
babies	feet	hours	nibble	smooth	want
baby	food	hunt	night	some	well
ball	for	in	not	south	what
birth	forests	is	now	stay	will
born	from	it	of	strong	with
branches	fruit	its	okay	that	would
bring	fruits	just	on	the	years
but	fur	leaves	one	their	you
by	get	lies	or	them	zoo
called	give	like	own	then	zookeepers
can	going	limbs	plants	they	zoos
central	grasp	live	plenty	think	

23

Fast Facts

Habitat: Tropical forests

Range: Central and South America

Average Length: Two-toed sloths, 21 to 29 inches (53 to 74 centimeters); three-toed sloths, 20 inches (51 centimeters)

Weight: Two-toed sloths, 9 to 18 pounds (4 to 8 kilograms); three-toed sloths, 7 to 11 pounds (3 to 5 kilograms)

Life Span: 25 to 30 years

Anatomy: Sloths have extremely long, curved claws that help them hang from branches.

Behavior: Sloths are very good swimmers.

Index